T0197527

William Gillette
Actor, Playwright, Inventor

Alison Berger

To order additional copies of this book, contact:
Xlibris
844-714-8691
www.Xlibris.com
Orders@Xlibris.com
or
Lamb Tales Books
1-860-449-8448
lambtalesedit@aol.com

Picture and Photo Credits
Cover; pages 1 to 15 (Aunt Polly), 23 (train), 24: public domain
Pages 15 (castle) to 23 (station): Alison Berger

ISBN: Softcover 978-1-4415-5895-4
ISBN: EBook 978-1-6641-8038-3

Print information available on the last page

Rev. date: 06/11/2021

William Gillette
Actor, Playwright, Inventor

Alison Berger

XLibris
1663 Liberty Drive Suite 200
Bloomington, Indiana 47403

Lamb Tales Books
Groton, Connecticut

Who was William Gillette?

"Elementary, [Watson], my dear fellow."

Many of you may have heard this famous expression of Sherlock Holmes. But you would probably be surprised to learn that it does not appear in any of the original stories written about him. Then where does it come from?

The character and adventures of the famous detective were born in the imagination of the author, Sir Arthur Conan Doyle. The man who helped bring Sherlock Holmes to life on the stage, on the radio, and in film was the American actor and playwright, William Gillette. Gillette wrote and starred in a play based closely on some of Doyle's stories.

Gillette coined the phrase "O, this is elementary, my dear fellow [Watson]." A later actor shortened it to "Elementary, my dear Watson."

Sherlock Holmes with his friend Dr. Watson

Gillette's family

William Gillette was born in Hartford, Connecticut, in 1853. His mother could trace her family line back to Thomas Hooker, the founder of Hartford. His father was a U.S. Senator active in politics.

William had three brothers and two sisters. His sister Mary died as a child. His oldest brother died of tuberculosis. The other brothers became involved in politics and the army. His second sister Elizabeth married.

In 1882, Gillette married Helen Nichols. The couple had a happy marriage until Helen died suddenly of a ruptured appendix. Gillette grieved for a long time, and later became ill with tuberculosis.

Helen Nichols Gillette

Gillette the actor

Gillette the writer and actor

Unlike his parents, brothers, and sisters, William left home for a career in the theater. He was twenty years old. Mark Twain saw promise in the young actor. "Apply for a part in my play, *Guilded Age*," Twain recommended.

Gillette wrote and starred in other successful plays, such as *Secret Service*. However, he is best known for his role as Sherlock Holmes. He starred in that role over 1300 times, both in the United States and Europe. In fact, his last tour as Holmes was in 1931, in the United States, at the age of seventy-six.

Gillette in *Secret Service*

During his career Gillette was one of the most important actors of his time. He appeared with such brilliant actors and actresses as Helen Hayes, Ethel Barrymore, Charles Coburn, and the young Charlie Chaplin.

Audiences enjoyed watching the thrilling narrow escapes that William Gillette the playwright devised for Holmes. Tall and slender with black hair and blue eyes, Mr. Gillette played the part of a quiet, intelligent, and resourceful man—especially as Sherlock Holmes. People often picture Holmes as a brilliant, reserved detective, with the hunting cap, long cape, and pipe. This image is due more to the actor William Gillette than to the author, Arthur Conan Doyle.

William Gillette with other
famous stage actors

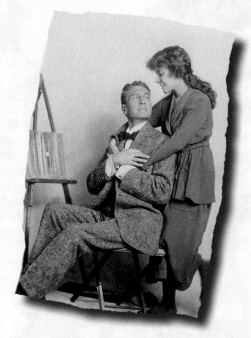

Gillette With Helen Hayes 1918

Gillette with Barrymore

The distinctive hunting cap

His inventions for the stage

Writing and acting were only two of William Gillette's many talents. He was an inventive genius. He improved sound systems, stage settings, and lighting. The stage technique of the fadeout when the lights dimmed then brightened again; the machine that reproduced the clattering of a horse's hooves; and the rainmaking machine that created the sound of rain splashing: all these are credited to Mr. Gillette.

Poster announces Gillette in *Secret Service*

Gillette Castle

This actor and inventor was as mysterious and unique a person as the character Sherlock Holmes. When he wasn't touring with his acting group, he spent most of his time on his houseboat, *Aunt Polly*. In 1914, Mr. Gillette began building a castle in Hadlyme, Connecticut, on a hill known as the Seventh Sister. He designed every detail of the building. This medieval castle is built on a natural rock formation overlooking the Connecticut River. Its twenty-four rooms display items from Gillette's past, as well as inventiveness and delight in the unique and curious.

The *Aunt Polly*

Gillette Castle

Each of the forty-seven doors inside the house is decorated with lovely carving. Yet, despite their number, no two doors have the same design.

Gillette set the dining room table on metal rollers and a track. This allowed him to have it moved away from the wall when he had guests, and then rolled back into place. He could call the butler by stepping on a certain board under the table. The pressure caused an electrical contact with the metal track, which in turn produced a call in the pantry.

First floor of Gillette Castle

These and other inventions were, in a sense, a hobby for Gillette. In his study the arm chair, like the dining room table, glides on metal rollers set in a track. The actor invented a complicated set of wooden locks. He was the only one who could open them.

William Gillette's study

Cats!

Another favorite and rather surprising occupation was cats—caring for live cats and collecting "cat art." A newspaperman once counted seventy-seven cats in Gillette's house. Seventeen were real while the rest were artwork: doorstops in the form of cats; ceramic cats; images of cats on the walls; and cat figures decorating the mantle. Many of Mr. Gillette's favorite live cats were professionally photographed. The prints were then mounted in a special cat scrapbook.

Cat figure outside the castle

His trains

Perhaps Mr. Gillette's most ambitious interest was building trains. He had a working railway system constructed on his Seventh Sister property. It included three miles of track, switches, trestles, stations, a roundhouse, a repair shop, and more. Two miniature locomotives—one driven by steam, the other by electricity—and two Pullmans ran on the tracks. Each carried seven passengers. An observation car held twenty-one. The actor delighted in taking his guests for a ride, whizzing around the curves, blasting the engine's whistle. After Gillette's death in 1937, an amusement park at Lake Compounce, Connecticut, bought the train, the track, and the equipment to use as a ride in the park.

Recently one of the original engines was beautifully restored and is on display in the Visitors' Center at Gillette Castle.

Gillette's Grand Central Station

Gillette's train

One of the
"Fifty Immortals"

The uniqueness of William Gillette's castle may impress some of the numerous visitors more than his life. But his real legacy, often forgotten or not known, lies in his great contribution to the acting profession. Gillette's particular gift consisted in bringing the exciting adventures of Sherlock Holmes to the stage, radio, and film.

In 1913, the National Institute of Arts and Letters named him one of the "Fifty Immortals."

The author of Sherlock Holmes's adventures, Sir Arthur Conan Doyle, kept in touch with Gillette. The Holmes in his stories, he once said, was "a very limp object compared with the glamour of your personality."

Gillette portrait

Gillette in action